KIDS FIGHT PLASTIC

How to Be a #2minutesuperhero

This is for you: the **#2minutesuperhero**

Text copyright © 2019 by Martin Dorey
Illustrations copyright © 2019 by Tim Wesson

First US edition 2020

Library of Congress Catalog Card Number pending
ISBN 978-1-5362-1277-8 (hardcover)
ISBN 978-1-5362-1587-8 (paperback)

20 21 22 23 24 25 LEO 10 9 8 7 6 5 4 3 2 1

Printed in Heshan, Guangdong, China

This book was typeset in Myriad Pro.
The illustrations were created digitally.

Candlewick Press
99 Dover Street
Somerville, Massachusetts 02144

www.candlewick.com

KIDS FIGHT PLASTIC

How to Be a #2minutesuperhero

MARTIN DOREY
ILLUSTRATED BY TIM WESSON

CANDLEWICK PRESS

CONTENTS

ARE YOU READY TO BE A SUPERHERO?

HOW TO BE A #2MINUTESUPERHERO

Have you got two minutes? Two minutes is all the time it takes to become a superhero. Not all superheroes fly or save the world from alien invaders. Some superheroes do simple, everyday things that take only a couple of minutes and add up to make a huge difference. These superheroes are just like you and me. They live among us, in secret, performing amazing feats. You can be one too.

WE NEED SUPERHEROES TO SAVE THE OCEAN

You are probably wondering why we need superheroes. It's simple. We need superheroes to **FIGHT PLASTIC** and **SAVE THE OCEAN**.

Our oceans are dying because we are using them as dumps by allowing them to fill with plastic. Our plastic waste is hurting the creatures that live in or around the ocean. If we don't watch out, plastic waste will hurt us too.

WE NEED SUPERHEROES LIKE YOU

Everything you do—good or bad—has an effect on the world around you. **FIGHTING PLASTIC** is a terrific way to change the world for the better.

Doing something simple for two minutes every day—such as picking up plastic litter—turns you into a superhero. Every small thing you do to fight plastic helps save the ocean. It also makes people around you take notice.

Politicians and big companies might say they care about fighting plastic, but in my experience, they take forever to take action, if they do anything at all.

So why wait?

YOU CAN FIGHT PLASTIC RIGHT NOW BY BECOMING A #2MINUTESUPERHERO.

WHY WE MUST FIGHT PLASTIC FOR THE OCEANS

- More than nine million tons (eight million metric tons) of plastic enter the oceans each year.

- Every square mile of ocean has 46,000 plastic items in it.

- Plastic is now present in every part of the ocean, including in the Arctic sea ice and at the bottom of the Mariana Trench, the deepest part of the world's oceans.

- It is estimated that by 2050 there will be more plastic (by mass) than fish in the oceans.

- Plastic does not biodegrade (break down into natural materials). All it does is break down into smaller and smaller pieces, known as microplastics.

- As plastic breaks down, it releases harmful chemicals that are believed to be contributing to climate change, the gradual warming of the planet due to human activity.

The oceans are vital to all of us, no matter where we live.

The oceans regulate our weather and make the air cleaner. They also provide us with half the oxygen we need to breathe to stay alive. And they absorb carbon dioxide, a gas that contributes to climate change and global warming.

The oceans provide food. Around 120 million tons (109 million metric tons) of fish are caught each year. Without this source of food, many people would starve.

The oceans are home to whales, dolphins, turtles, otters, seals, fish, sharks, rays, plankton, manatees, lobsters, crabs, and jellyfish, as well as seaweeds, grasses, and algae.

The oceans are a fantastic, vast, and wonderful playground for swimming, snorkeling, splashing, and surfing!

We have to look after them.

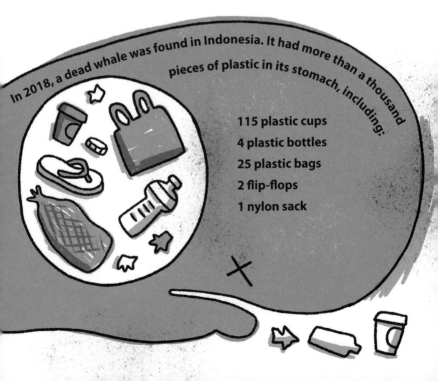

In 2018, a dead whale was found in Indonesia. It had more than a thousand pieces of plastic in its stomach, including:

115 plastic cups
4 plastic bottles
25 plastic bags
2 flip-flops
1 nylon sack

WHY WE MUST FIGHT PLASTIC FOR WILDLIFE

SOMETHING'S FISHY: Studies show up to 90 percent of seabirds have plastic in their stomachs.

- Plastic entanglement: estimates suggest 100,000 sea creatures—whales, dolphins, and turtles—and 1 million seabirds die each year because of plastic entanglement or ingestion.

- Lost plastic fishing gear entangles and kills hundreds of thousands of fish and animals each year.

- Tiny organisms called algae grow on plastic in seawater. The algae give off chemicals that confuse the seabirds into thinking the plastic is food. Seabirds that eat plastic die hungry, unable to digest it. Chicks with stomachs full of plastic can't fledge (learn to fly), so they are stuck on the water.

- Fish mistake tiny pieces of plastic for food, eat them, and starve. If we eat fish, there is also the chance that we could end up eating the plastic the fish have eaten.

- Plastic attracts persistent organic pollutants (POPs) in seawater. These chemicals build up on plastic, becoming more and more toxic. The POPs can then bioaccumulate up the food chain. This means that if a big fish eats a little fish, it absorbs the toxins. Then when that fish gets eaten by a bigger fish, the toxins pass on to that fish! In theory, these toxic chemicals could enter the human food chain.

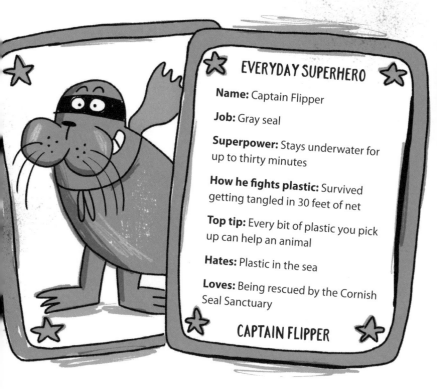

EVERYDAY SUPERHERO

Name: Captain Flipper

Job: Gray seal

Superpower: Stays underwater for up to thirty minutes

How he fights plastic: Survived getting tangled in 30 feet of net

Top tip: Every bit of plastic you pick up can help an animal

Hates: Plastic in the sea

Loves: Being rescued by the Cornish Seal Sanctuary

CAPTAIN FLIPPER

MEET THE EVERYDAY SUPERHEROES

Don't despair! Superheroes live among us, even if they don't have flashy costumes or their own TV shows. They fight plastic because they believe it's the right thing to do or because they need to survive. You're going to meet some real-life everyday superheroes in this book. I hope they inspire you to become a superhero too.

MARTIN AND HIS #2MINUTE MISSION

Let me tell you a bit about me. My name is Martin, and I'm going to train you to become a **#2minutesuperhero**. I hate trash, particularly plastic waste, and I think there are lots of ways we can fight plastic in our lives.

I live on the coast, and my town has a beach. Trash washes up onto the beach with every tide. After storms, the amount of trash can be heartbreaking. I go and pick it up, but I know that there will always be more. So I need help.

The more you fight plastic, the more you help the ocean, my beach, and beaches all over the world. Wherever you live, you are connected to the ocean by rivers, waterways, sewers, and drains. If we stop plastic from getting into the water, we stop it from washing up on the beach.

EVERYDAY SUPERHERO

Name: Martin

Job: Writer and activist

Superpower: Writes about plastic to help people make changes

How he fights plastic: Started the **#2minutebeachclean** movement

Top tip: Every single person can make a difference

Hates: Fishing waste

Loves: Clean beaches

MARTIN

THE #2MINUTEBEACHCLEAN

In 2013, I decided to do something about the trash on my beach. I quickly picked up some trash and took a picture of it. I posted my picture online using a brand-new hashtag, **#2minutebeachclean**, hoping someone might see it and take two minutes to do the same thing.

Amazingly, they did. By spring 2019, there were more than 120,000 pictures of people picking up litter posted on Instagram from all over the world.

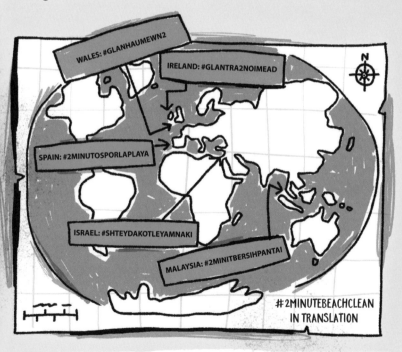

WALES: #GLANHAUMEWN2

IRELAND: #GLANTRA2NOIMEAD

SPAIN: #2MINUTOSPORLAPLAYA

ISRAEL: #SHTEYDAKOTLEYAMNAKI

MALAYSIA: #2MINITBERSIHPANTAI

#2MINUTEBEACHCLEAN IN TRANSLATION

ANALYTIC PLASTIC: It is estimated that each **#2minutebeachclean** weighs more than 4 pounds (2 kilograms), which means that at least 240 tons (218 metric tons) of litter have been picked up since 2013.

HOW TO USE THIS BOOK

- This book is separated into **MISSIONS**, which are all about the areas of your life where you can fight plastic, how you can do it, and why it's important.

- Within each larger mission, you'll also find a series of **2-MINUTE MISSIONS**. These are tasks that I want you to complete. Each of them is worth **SUPERHERO POINTS**.

- Some missions are easy! Some missions are hard (and may take more than two minutes, to be honest!), but they will earn you more points. You might need an adult to help.

- As you complete each mission, note how many points you have scored.

- Once you reach the end of the book—and the end of your superhero training—you can calculate your final score. This will give you a **SUPERHERO RATING**.

What kind of **#2minutesuperhero** will you be?

SUPERHERO STAT: Nine out of ten superheroes don't even know they are superheroes yet.

READY FOR ACTION?

Before you begin your first mission, I need you to make this promise.

I solemnly swear to pledge my allegiance to the ocean.

I will take care of the ocean through my everyday actions and will use two minutes of each day to fight plastic.

Training approved by:

Founder of the #2minutebeachclean

THE #2MINUTESUPERHERO RULES

Fighting plastic isn't impossible. You can do it. But at some point or other, you are going to have to pick up someone else's litter. It's horrible, but it must be done! To keep you safe, here are some rules you have to follow.

YOUR MISSIONS START NOW

GET TO KNOW THE BAD STUFF

Let's start your training by learning about the bad stuff. Your first mission is to get to know about plastic and, in particular, single-use plastic. That's the plastic that gets used just once and then thrown away. That's the bad stuff we want to fight. The good stuff, on the other hand, makes toys, gadgets, and life-saving medical equipment, and is used for long periods of time.

THE HISTORY OF PLASTIC

Plastic—in some form or other—has been around for a long time. It can be molded or shaped, making it an incredibly useful material for all kinds of things, from computers and cables to toys and medical equipment.

The first plastic to be made from oil was invented about one hundred years ago. It was called Bakelite, and you can still find it in old houses (look for brown light switches). Since then, our world has become more and more reliant on oil-based plastic.

Over the last hundred years, different types of plastic have been invented for all kinds of uses: Plexiglas is clear and replaces glass for windows. Polypropylene makes syringes for injections. High-density polyethylene makes plastic bags and milk bottles. Nylon makes clothes, carpets, and nets.

IDENTIFYING PLASTICS

Most plastic items you buy new will have a symbol on them that says what type of plastic the item is made from. Different plastics have different properties. Some plastics float in water; others don't. Some can be recycled, while others can't. Some are more toxic than others.

CODE AND SYMBOL	PLASTIC TYPE	TYPICALLY USED FOR	PROPERTIES
01 PET	Polyethylene terephthalate	Soft-drink bottles, peanut-butter jars	RECYCLABLE Clear, tough, sinks in water
02 HDPE	High-density polyethylene	Shopping bags, milk jugs, detergent bottles	RECYCLABLE Floats in water
03 PVC	Polyvinyl chloride	Blister packs, pipes and hoses, clear food packaging	NOT EASY TO RECYCLE Considered to be the most toxic of all plastics
04 LDPE	Low-density polyethylene	Garbage bags, squeezable bottles, cling wrap	NOT EASY TO RECYCLE Floats in water
05 PP	Polypropylene	Bottle caps, straws, yogurt containers, syringes	NOT EASY TO RECYCLE Floats in water
06 PS 06 PS-E	Polystyrene, expanded polystyrene	Plastic cutlery, packing peanuts, toys	NOT EASY TO RECYCLE Releases chemicals that are believed to cause cancer
07 OTHER	Polycarbonate resins and composite material	Components, computers, electronics	NOT EASY TO RECYCLE Any plastics that can't be categorized by the other six. Often toxic.

WHEN PLASTIC IS GOOD

Plastic is fantastic. It is light, strong, and cheap, which means lots of things are made from it. Toys, such as Lego bricks, *Star Wars* figures, dolls, and Xboxes, are all made from plastic.

It's durable, too, so it doesn't rust or decay like metal or wood. It will last in some form for hundreds of years, which makes it a practical choice of material. Plastic can also be reused many times. Some types are recyclable.

Medical equipment is often made from plastic. In fact, some advances in medicine wouldn't have happened without plastic. Lots of people who need assistive devices, medication, or medical equipment rely on plastic to live better lives.

SURPRISING PLASTICS

Tea bags often have plastic in them.

Chip bags are made from plastic.

Most diapers are made from plastic.

YOUR 2-MINUTE MISSION: **Find five pieces of good plastic that you use every day.**
10 POINTS

WHEN PLASTIC IS BAD

One of the problems with plastic is that it is made from oil, which takes millions of years to form. Oil is a nonrenewable resource, so once we've used it all up, it's gone and we can't make more of it.

The other problem is that plastic is durable. It doesn't biodegrade like wood, or rust away into nontoxic materials. It is PERSISTENT. Unless we do something with it, plastic will never go away. If it does break down—because it's been in the sea or in the ground—it just breaks down into smaller and smaller pieces, releasing chemicals that are bad for the planet in the process.

Plastic has become one of the most-used materials on the planet, but we haven't yet figured out what to do when we've finished with it! D'oh!

We're the ones who allow it to persist in the environment by letting it flow into the sea or burying it in landfill. So maybe it's not plastic itself that's bad. Maybe it's the way we use plastic in our daily lives—without thinking about it—that's the problem.

YOUR 2-MINUTE MISSION: **Find five pieces of bad plastic that will be used only once before being thrown away. 20 POINTS**

1907

The first synthetic plastic to be made from oil— Bakelite—is created.

1930

Scotch tape is invented.

2004

The term *microplastics* is first used to describe tiny plastic particles that pollute the environment.

1976

Plastic becomes one of the most-used materials in the world.

2009

The Boeing 787 airplane is made from 50 percent plastic.

2015

An oceanographer films a turtle with a straw up its nose.

2017

The documentary *Blue Planet II* opens the world's eyes to the problem of plastic.

1941

The first polyester fiber, Terylene, is kept secret because of World War II.

1958

Plastic Lego bricks are invented.

1969

Neil Armstrong plants a nylon flag on the moon.

EVERYDAY SUPERHERO

Name: Rob

Job: Underwater trash collector

Superpower: Transforms plastic fishing nets into kayaks

How he fights plastic: Runs a diving group that collects plastic on the seabed

Top tip: Shout about plastic pollution

Hates: The idea that single-use plastic is OK

Loves: Turning old plastic into something useful

ROB

FIGHT PLASTIC IN YOUR TRASH CAN

I love talking trash. But not because I like seeing it! It's because I like figuring out what I should do with it. If you're going to fight plastic—and become a #2minutesuperhero— you're going to have to get to know your garbage can!

WHAT'S IN OUR WASTE?

- The US produces around 262 million tons (238 million metric tons) of household waste each year.

- The average person in the US produces around 1,600 pounds (726 kilograms) of waste per year.

- On average, around 35 percent of that waste gets recycled or composted.

- Only 9 percent of plastic gets recycled.

- The amount of plastic waste generated annually in the US is estimated to be about 35 million tons (32 million metric tons).

WHAT HAPPENS TO YOUR WASTE?

You put things in the trash and then forget about them. Off they go, and that's that. Sadly, it's not. Everything has to go somewhere. But where? There is no "away" to throw stuff into. We need to think carefully about what happens to the waste in our household trash.

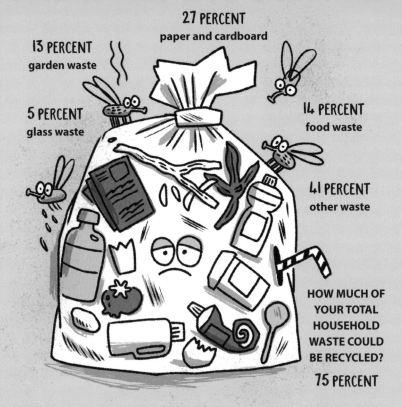

27 PERCENT
paper and cardboard

13 PERCENT
garden waste

5 PERCENT
glass waste

14 PERCENT
food waste

41 PERCENT
other waste

HOW MUCH OF
YOUR TOTAL
HOUSEHOLD
WASTE COULD
BE RECYCLED?

75 PERCENT

WHAT HAPPENS TO FOOD AND GARDEN WASTE?

Food and garden waste is organic matter and can be put into
a home compost bin. It will break down into a concoction
of natural materials, known as compost, that will benefit the
planet and help new life to grow. Amazing!

Some towns collect food and garden waste for
composting.

YOUR 2-MINUTE MISSION: **Get a food-waste bin and start
a compost heap! Find out how to make compost in
Mission 8.**
30 POINTS

WHAT HAPPENS TO YOUR HOUSEHOLD WASTE?

If you put stuff in your recycling bin, it will go to:

- a materials recovery facility (MRF), where it is sorted into recyclable and nonrecyclable waste.

If you put stuff in your household trash can, it will either go to:

- a landfill, a hole in the ground where it may leak chemicals and greenhouse gases (the gases that contribute to global warming and climate change). Not good!

or:

- energy recovery, which is when waste is burned to make electricity. This is good because waste is turned into useful energy, but bad because some of it could have been recycled.

> **YOUR 2-MINUTE MISSION:** Make a trash chart and mark it each time anyone takes out the trash. Monitor how many trash bags your family puts out each week and see if you can cut it in half.
> **50 POINTS**

WHAT HAPPENS TO YOUR RECYCLABLE WASTE?

Recyclable waste—which you sort into your recycling bin—is collected and turned into something else. Or so you thought!

It's silly, but recycling doesn't always get recycled. It all depends on the quality of recycling (how clean it is), the type of materials (some plastics are worth more than others), and the value of each material.

Basically, some recycling gets recycled. Some doesn't.

Confusing? Yup. While recycling is VITAL, it is not always the best way to fight plastic.

The best way? Say no to single-use plastic. Reuse stuff. Reduce the amount of stuff you have. Repair your stuff!

> **RECYCLING THE FACTS:** Until 2017, the US shipped a lot of recycling to China. Now China no longer takes it, which means it has to go somewhere else. It may end up in a landfill or the ocean.

> **YOUR 2-MINUTE MISSION:** Visit a materials recovery facility (MRF) near you.
> **50 POINTS**

WHAT ABOUT BIODEGRADABLE AND COMPOSTABLE PLASTICS?

Some companies have developed plastic alternatives that are supposedly compostable or biodegradable.

If something is labeled compostable, it will break down—like food waste. But often compostable packaging will break down only under certain conditions in industrial composters at the right temperature. Another problem is that if you throw compostable waste in the recycling bin, it can ruin the recycling.

Biodegradable items, such as some straws and cutlery, will break down eventually into organic matter, but often this has to happen under controlled conditions in a special facility.

New plastics, or bioplastics, are being developed from anything from sugar cane to soy. The great thing about them is that they aren't made from oil and don't leave nasty chemicals when they degrade. The downside is that unless they are disposed of properly, they can be as persistent as normal plastic.

I know! My head is about to explode too.

YOUR 2-MINUTE MISSION: **Find three straws—one that is plastic, one that is biodegradable plastic, and one that is paper. Get a plant pot and fill it with mud. Then poke the straws halfway into the mud. Leave them for a couple of weeks and see what happens!**
20 POINTS

WHAT HAPPENS TO WASTE IN OTHER COUNTRIES?

In some countries where they don't have recycling plants or refuse collections, garbage gets put into dumps and burned; thrown into rivers, where it ends up in the ocean; or just left to rot (or not, if it's plastic). And littering is a problem across the world. Many countries and cities are trying to keep trash from piling up in the streets and fields by taking steps to ban single-use plastic. Hurrah!

KENYA
Banned plastic bags in 2017 with heavy fines for anyone making, selling, or using a plastic bag

MOROCCO
Banned plastic bags in 2016

VANUATU
Banned plastic bags and straws and Styrofoam food containers in 2019

FRANCE
Banned plastic bags in 2016 and plastic cutlery, plates, and cups in 2020

ZIMBABWE
Banned all Styrofoam food containers in 2017

RWANDA
Banned plastic bags in 2008

DELHI (INDIA)
Banned disposable plastic in 2017

VANCOUVER (CANADA)
Banned plastic bags, Styrofoam food containers, and plastic straws in 2020

FIGHT PLASTIC IN YOUR PARK

How often do you go to the park? Do you ever see litter? What about that plastic bottle you see out of the corner of your eye when you fly down the slide? You know the one!

Do you ever imagine that a piece of litter, left in your park or street, could find its way to the sea? It can! All plastic in the ocean comes from somewhere—and you don't want it to come from your park. Right? This is why your BIG fight against plastic starts right here, right now, in your street, park, or school playground.

YOUR 2-MINUTE MISSION: Do a #2minutelitterpick. On your walk home from school or at the park, spend two minutes filling an old tote bag with litter. Recycle what you can, and trash the rest. How much did you get in two minutes?
20 POINTS

HOW THE PLASTIC IN YOUR PARK GETS IN THE OCEAN

Believe it or not, your park, street, or playground is connected to the ocean. All drains lead to sewers, streams, or rivers that, in turn, lead to the ocean.

The trash that your family—and all the other families on your street—discards every week also has a route to the ocean. If your trash bags burst open or your garbage can blows over and spills plastic in your street, it can be blown into a drain or river and then be carried out to sea. The same happens with litter.

If you keep your street, playground, or park plastic-free, then you'll be helping to look after the oceans.

That's why YOU are important in the fight against plastic.

⭐ EVERYDAY SUPERHERO

Name: Neil

Job: Litter picker

Superpower: Keeps the country tidy

How he fights plastic: Picks up litter anywhere and everywhere he can

Top tip: Stay positive. We can do this!

Hates: When people watch you pick up litter but don't help

Loves: The warm, fuzzy feeling of seeing a clean beach

NEIL

1. Overflowing garbage cans
2. Litter dropped in towns and cities
3. Litter left on the beach
4. Released accidentally by factories
5. Released as microfibers when clothes are washed
6. Products that are flushed down toilets and into the sewage system
7. Lost fishing equipment
8. Dumped as waste by ships or fishing boats
9. Lost shipping containers
10. Badly managed garbage dumps

MISSION 4

FIGHT PLASTIC IN YOUR BACKPACK

What do superheroes keep in their backpacks?
Can I guess? I bet you have a couple of pencils in there.
But how about felt-tip or ballpoint pens? What about
empty chip bags? School books? Textbooks? A ruler? Candy
wrappers? An odd glove, perhaps. And definitely a reusable
water bottle. Am I right? This mission is going to help you
remove unnecessary plastic from your backpack.

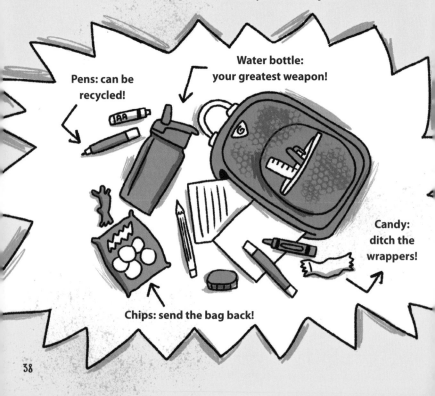

Pens: can be recycled!

Water bottle:
your greatest weapon!

Candy:
ditch the
wrappers!

Chips: send the bag back!

BUST THE BALLPOINTS

Did you know that around 15 million ballpoint pens are sold around the world every day? Ballpoint pens are made of plastic and metal and are hard to recycle. Many pens are designed to be disposable—when they run out, you throw them away. It's up to you to ensure they don't end up in a landfill.

A TRAIL OF WASTE:

Between 1950 and 2005, Bic, one of the world's biggest makers of pens, sold more than 100 billion plastic ballpoint pens. That's enough to draw a line to the moon and back more than 320,000 times.

Power to the pen!

YOUR 2-MINUTE MISSION:

Have a pen amnesty! Ask all your friends to empty their schoolbags and collect their old pens. Then ask a teacher or parent to help you raise money for a zero-waste box at www.terracycle.com. You can send your pens to them for recycling.
80 POINTS

WHY YOUR WATER BOTTLE IS THE BEST THING EVER!

Your reusable water bottle is your best weapon in the fight against plastic. Every time you refill it, you are doing something great. So keep it up! Turn on the tap, reduce your plastic waste, and help the ocean.

- You are likely to go to school for 180 days a year for thirteen years. If you use a reusable water bottle instead of a disposable one every day, you are saving 2,340 bottles over the course of your school life.

- Tap water is 600 times cheaper than bottled water, and for you, at school, it's FREE.

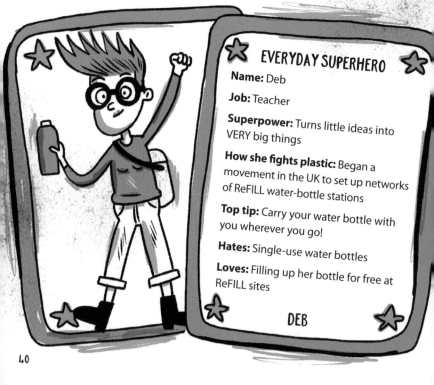

EVERYDAY SUPERHERO

Name: Deb

Job: Teacher

Superpower: Turns little ideas into VERY big things

How she fights plastic: Began a movement in the UK to set up networks of ReFILL water-bottle stations

Top tip: Carry your water bottle with you wherever you go!

Hates: Single-use water bottles

Loves: Filling up her bottle for free at ReFILL sites

DEB

- Tap water is healthier than soft drinks.

- You can drink as much tap water as you want. Keep filling that bottle!

- Plastic bottles and bottle tops make up 15 percent of beach litter.

- Most plastic bottles don't float (unless they have a top), so they sink to the bottom of the ocean, where they remain on the seabed.

- On the seabed, a bottle can break down into thousands of pieces of microplastic.

- 50 billion plastic bottles get used every day in the US.

- Only about 23 percent of plastic bottles get recycled.

YOUR 2-MINUTE MISSION:
Does your school have a water fountain where you can fill your water bottle? Fill up! If not, how about starting a petition for a fountain or bottle-refilling station at school? You could ask your parents and friends' parents to sign it too!
30 POINTS

THOSE PESKY CANDY WRAPPERS

Back to your backpack. How many old candy wrappers did you find in there?

The bad news: Did you know that a lot of candy wrappers can't be recycled because of what they are made from? It's not great news, especially as superheroes need a little sugar rush every so often. (In moderation, of course.)

The good news: You don't have to have candy in plastic wrappers! Some still come in cardboard or foil. Bulk candy can sometimes be bought in paper bags, and some mints come in handy tins. The tins keep the mints from getting fluffy, are plastic-free, and can be used to store all your little stuff in them afterward. Genius.

YOUR 2-MINUTE MISSION: **Sadly, if it comes wrapped in plastic, it may be time to stop buying your old candy. But it's also time to go candy shopping. Get yourself some mints in a tin! Look for candy sold in cardboard! 10 POINTS**

CHIPS

Am I right in thinking you've had a bag of chips recently? What did you do with the bag afterward? Toss it? Sadly, until now, that was the only thing we could do with them.

The bad news: Chip bags are REALLY hard to recycle because they are made from plastic and foil. Most of them go into the landfill. Shocked? Wait till you see the stats.

The worst news: Lays, one of the world's biggest chip manufacturers, sells more than 372 million bags of chips a year. That's 1,416 bags every two minutes.

The good news: TerraCycle has a zero-waste box for snack wrappers, including chip bags and chocolate-bar wrappers. Now you can collect them, send them back, and know they will be turned into something else.

YOUR 2-MINUTE MISSION: **Collect all your chip bags. Collect all your friends' bags. With help from a parent or teacher, set up a chip-bag recycling point and raise money for a zero-waste box. Send the bags off to be recycled. Find out more at www.terracycle.com. 80 POINTS**

FIGHT PLASTIC IN YOUR LUNCHROOM

When plastic affects us personally, it can be hard to make changes, especially if it means giving up tasty things you love. If your lunch is packed with good stuff but packaged in plastic, you are going to have to make some difficult decisions. Are you ready to fight for your lunch? You are? Superhero status awaits!

EVERYDAY SUPERHERO

Name: Helford the Hero

Job: Common dolphin

Superpower: Super intelligence

How she fights plastic: Fought a plastic fishing line for hours before she was rescued

Top tip: Eat only fish that has been caught using dolphin-friendly nets

Hates: Humans leaving fishing nets in the sea

Loves: Playing with her pod

HELFORD THE HERO

TAKE A LOOK AT YOUR LUNCH

Superheroes eat lunch. That's a fact. But what's it packaged in? Does your lunch come with a plastic fork? On a plastic plate? With chips? Do you have juice in a juice box, with a straw? Do your carrots come ready-cut in a plastic bag? It might be time for a change.

YOUR 2-MINUTE MISSION: At your next lunch break, ask three friends to show you their lunches. Show them yours. Do your lunches contain plastic? Make a vow to cut out AT LEAST one piece of plastic from lunch. 10 POINTS

So I hear you've been PACKING PLASTIC, Mr. Lunchbox!

TAKE CONTROL OF YOUR PACKED LUNCH

Making packed lunches every day takes time and effort.
Often the easiest options are the worst for the planet.

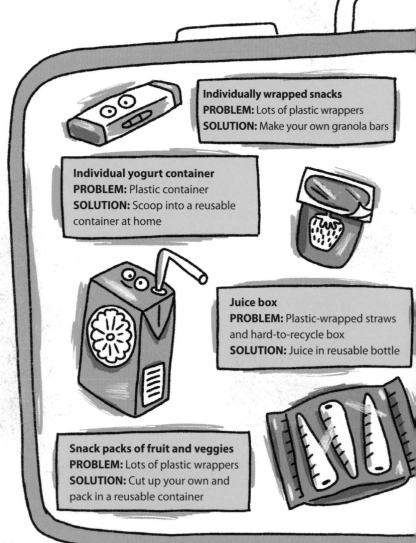

Individually wrapped snacks
PROBLEM: Lots of plastic wrappers
SOLUTION: Make your own granola bars

Individual yogurt container
PROBLEM: Plastic container
SOLUTION: Scoop into a reusable
container at home

Juice box
PROBLEM: Plastic-wrapped straws
and hard-to-recycle box
SOLUTION: Juice in reusable bottle

Snack packs of fruit and veggies
PROBLEM: Lots of plastic wrappers
SOLUTION: Cut up your own and
pack in a reusable container

Pre-cut apples, snack-size chocolate bars, sandwiches, salads, and drinks usually come packaged in lots of plastic.

Sandwiches in plastic wrap
PROBLEM: Plastic wrap can't be recycled
SOLUTION: Bring your own in a reusable container or beeswax wrap (see Mission 7)

Bottled soda
PROBLEM: Plastic bottle
SOLUTION: Reusable drink bottle

Box of salad
PROBLEM: Clear wrapper may not be recyclable
SOLUTION: Make your own and pack it in a reusable container

FIGHT PLASTIC IN YOUR SCHOOL LUNCH

How many school lunches get served in your school each day? If your school lunches get served with single-use plastic straws, plastic cutlery, cartons, plastic bottles, or plastic containers, then it's not hard to do the math and figure out how much plastic your school could save by changing to non-plastic alternatives.

It's time to fight for a plastic-free lunch!

Imagine how many lunches are served in your school over a school year.

Then imagine how many schools there are in the whole country.

YOUR 2-MINUTE MISSION: Show and tell! Ask your teacher if you can talk to your class or in assembly about your #2minutesuperhero mission. Explain why you are trying to reduce plastic and how you are doing it. Ask your fellow students to sign a pledge to help you.
50 POINTS

Think about how many
millions of school lunches
are eaten every year.

And remember, it
takes only one plastic
straw to kill a turtle.

YOUR 2-MINUTE MISSION: **Does your school have a recycling point for single-use plastics such as yogurt containers, straws, and drink bottles? If not, set one up! Get permission from your teacher and principal. Make labels so everyone can see what goes where. 40 POINTS**

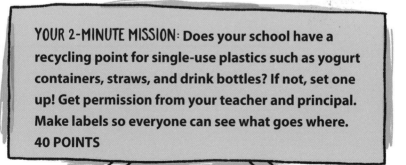

FIGHT PLASTIC IN THE SUPERMARKET

This is where the fight against plastic gets serious. Why? Because foods and drinks are major sources of single-use packaging. Reducing our reliance on single-use plastic packaging in the supermarket is a huge step in the fight against plastic. But don't worry, I will try to keep this part of your training fun. And short.

WHY DO SUPERMARKETS USE SO MUCH PLASTIC?

Supermarkets are full of plastic packaging for lots of reasons.

HYGIENE
Packaging keeps food free from germs.

FRESHNESS
Some food will last longer if it is wrapped in plastic.

TRANSPORTATION
Our food comes from all over the world.

PERFECTION
We like our food to look its best.

HOW CAN YOU AVOID PLASTIC IN FOOD?

- Choose plastic-free fruits and vegetables
- Buy from local shops
- Buy from farmers' markets
- Bring your own containers to the supermarket deli counter
- Always bring your reusable bags!

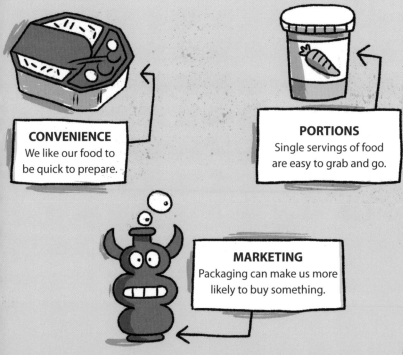

CONVENIENCE
We like our food to be quick to prepare.

PORTIONS
Single servings of food are easy to grab and go.

MARKETING
Packaging can make us more likely to buy something.

FIGHT PLASTIC WITH PESTER POWER

Do your parents take you with them when they go to the supermarket? Good! Superheroes love it because it's a chance to get involved with the shopping. Pester your parents! Make a nuisance of yourself so that your family makes the best possible choices when it comes to food. If there's an alternative that's not wrapped in plastic, get them to join you in your fight by changing what they buy!

YOUR 2-MINUTE MISSION:
Offer to help with the shopping so that you'll have a say in the food you buy as a family.
20 POINTS

FIGHT PLASTIC BY MAKING SHOPPING DIFFERENT

Supermarkets are difficult places to fight plastic. So maybe it's time to go somewhere else! Farmers' markets are much more fun and are great places to buy fresh and local vegetables without all the wrapping.

You could also take your folks to a store that sells food in bulk, where you'll be able to pick up lots of dried goods, like flour, sugar, salt, and grains, without any kind of packaging. Don't forget your old takeout containers!

YOUR 2-MINUTE MISSION: **Go on a plastic-free shopping trip and come back with ZERO waste! 40 POINTS**

MISSION 7

FIGHT PLASTIC IN YOUR KITCHEN

Who runs the kitchen in your house? If you are really going to fight plastic in the kitchen, you might need to stage a kitchen takeover. There are lots of things you can do to fight plastic in the kitchen. You can avoid food that comes in plastic, dabble in a bit of dishwashing, start a VERY strict plastic-bag policy, learn to cook without plastic, and help your family make better, plastic-free choices.

MAKE YOUR KITCHEN A BAG-FREE ZONE

How many bags are there under your kitchen sink? I bet there are tons!

It's your job to swap them for canvas bags you can use again and again. Don't let your family use anything else.

In 2016, California banned most stores from handing out single-use plastic bags. Before this ban, California retailers gave out more than 19 billion bags every year. Volunteers collecting trash in Monterey County found only 43 plastic bags in 2017, compared to almost 2,500 in 2010.

This shows that small changes and actions can add up to make a BIG difference. Go, us!

YOUR 2-MINUTE MISSION: Become the bag police! Announce a zero-tolerance plastic grocery-bag policy. Make sure every member of your family has NO EXCUSE for using a plastic bag. Put canvas bags in the car, under the sink, and always close by, then charge each family member 10¢ for every plastic grocery bag they use.
20 POINTS

EVERYDAY SUPERHERO

Name: Jim

Job: Lifeguard

Superpower: Drives a Jet Ski

How he fights plastic: Held a fourteen-hour beach cleanup from dawn until dusk

Top tip: Ditch plastic bags. They get caught in Jet Ski engines, making it harder to rescue people.

Hates: Plastic bags. You don't need them!

Loves: Telling people about the problems with single-use plastic

JIM

FREE THE SINK FROM PLASTIC

Dishwashing intervention! Does your family use sponges or scrubbers or buy dish soap? That's your chance to fight plastic! Most sponges are made from plastic, so every time you use them, tiny bits of plastic go down the sink and eventually into the ocean. Every time you use a sponge or a synthetic cloth, you risk washing hundreds of tiny plastic fibers into the ocean.

YOUR 2-MINUTE MISSION: **Trade plastic scrubbers for coconut-husk or metal ones and refill your dish-soap bottle at a store that sells in bulk.**
30 POINTS

FIGHT PLASTIC WITH YOUR SUPERHERO SAUCEPAN

Can you cook? It might be time to learn. Cooking with fresh ingredients (that don't come in plastic packaging) is much better for the planet than eating food that comes in tons of packaging, like premade dinners, cups of soup, or salads in plastic bags. Cook with loose vegetables, and you'll reduce your plastic consumption right away. Learning to bake cakes, bread, and pizza will also help with your plastic consumption. And cooking can be a lot of fun, too!

GIVE UP THE MINI PORTIONS

Food that comes in individual portions—like small containers of yogurt and snack-size food—uses more than double the amount of plastic than larger containers. Say no! You can scoop yogurt out of a big container, eat cookies from a large pack, and have cereal from a giant box. Easy!

YOUR 2-MINUTE MISSION: **Choose your favorite cereal. Find the biggest and smallest boxes of it that you can. Figure out how many bowls of cereal each box contains and how many boxes of each size you'd need to fill 100 bowls.**
10 POINTS

FIGHT THE PLASTIC WRAP

How about having a fun afternoon making an alternative to plastic wrap that's 100 percent natural, reusable, easy to make, and keeps food just as fresh for just as long?

YOUR 2-MINUTE MISSION: Make beeswax wraps with an adult. Find your brightest cotton fabric and paint it with beeswax (buy it online). If you are vegan, use plant-based wax. You can add pine resin to make the wraps sticky.
40 POINTS

HOW TO MAKE BEESWAX WRAPS

1. Get an adult to help. Cut 10-inch (25-centimeter) squares out of old washed cotton fabric.
2. Put one square of fabric on a baking tray lined with parchment. Sprinkle with 2 teaspoons of beeswax beads.
3. Carefully put the baking tray in a preheated oven (around 200°F/100°C) for five to ten minutes.
4. Using oven mitts, take the tray out of the oven. Use a paintbrush to spread the wax over the fabric. Remove the fabric by attaching two clothespins to the top corners.
5. Hold the fabric over the tray for two minutes to let it cool.
6. Leave it to dry on a wire tray for five minutes.
7. After you've used the wrap, wash in cool water, then be awesome and reuse!

FIGHT PLASTIC IN YOUR GARDEN

Are you ready to get mucky? Superheroes with green thumbs are going to love this mission. Why? Because it's all about fighting plastic in your yard and how you can use old plastic to grow new plants. And it's going to get messy. Hooray!

MAKING COMPOST

Compost is the best kind of material for growing plants. Plants love it because it's made from rotted-down matter that is full of natural goodness.

It's easy to make compost at home if you have space, although it does take time—more than two minutes!

If you can't make your own, you can sometimes buy it from your town. It will be made from food and garden waste that gets collected from your community. Sometimes it's free!

HOW TO MAKE COMPOST

1. Get a compost bin from your town or make your own.

2. Collect your vegetable peelings, as well as green and brown matter from your garden.

3. Put it in your compost bin.

4. Turn it over every couple of weeks to help it rot.

5. Ta-da! Compost!

SAVING PLASTIC BY GROWING

Growing plants is fun and often easier than you think. And growing your own can save you from having to buy vegetables at the supermarket. A lot of store-bought salad comes in bags or wrappers that cannot be recycled, so it makes good sense to grow vegetables at home so you can cut down on plastic waste. Plus it's good for you. And tasty too.

HOW TO GROW LETTUCE AT HOME

1. Get some mixed lettuce seeds.

2. Fill a large, clean black plastic food carton with compost.

3. Spread the seeds across the top. Cover with another thin layer of compost.

4. Place on a sunny windowsill. Water gently. Wait for about ten days. Water as needed.

5. Cut the lettuce leaves when they are small. Leave them to grow some more. Cut again.

REUSING PLASTIC

Sadly, there is still a lot of single-use plastic out there. Gardening is a great way to reuse it. Yogurt containers, plastic food containers, and plastic bottles are all perfect for growing seeds.

YOUR 2-MINUTE MISSION: **Cut a clear plastic bottle in half and fill the bottom with compost. Insert three pea seeds into the compost around the bottle's edge. Water and leave on a windowsill. You'll be able to see the seeds germinate and the seedlings grow. When they're big enough, plant them outside in a larger pot. Enjoy fresh pea shoots in your salad or wait to eat the peas. 20 POINTS**

★ EVERYDAY SUPERHERO ★

Name: Dr. Seaweed

Job: Gardener

Superpower: Green thumb

How she fights plastic: Reusing plastic pots and containers in her garden

Top tip: Start a compost heap so you can grow plants from your old vegetable peelings

Hates: Waste that doesn't get used up

Loves: Seeing new life grow

DR. SEAWEED

START A GARDENING CLUB

If you can't start a garden at home, get help starting a gardening club at school or in your community. Start small by planting simple vegetables, such as tomatoes, and then move on from there!

YOUR 2-MINUTE MISSION: Talk to your teacher about starting a gardening club or growing vegetables in your classroom. Bring in leftover plastic pots, trays, and containers, and then take the vegetables home when they're big enough to eat.

20 POINTS

FIGHT PLASTIC IN YOUR BATHROOM

The bathroom is a great place to fight plastic. Why? Because there is so much of it in there! Many bathroom products, from soap to shampoo, are either made from or come packaged in plastic. It might seem like a difficult task to switch to something that isn't plastic, but it can be done! In fact, these two-minute missions are easier than you might think.

BATHROOM PLASTICS LAID BARE

- Every year in the US we dispose of up to one billion toothbrushes!

- The US goes through 83,000 tons (77,000 metric tons) of disposable wipes a year.

- Cotton-swab sticks are often found on beach cleans. They are small enough to escape the sewage system and get washed out to sea.

Toothbrushes are almost always plastic. But they don't have to be.

Toothpaste usually comes in plastic tubes. Again, it doesn't have to. Some brands come in metal tubes that can easily be recycled, and some come in tablet form or in glass jars.

Liquid soap comes in plastic bottles—some can be refilled, while others just get thrown away or recycled when they are empty. Also, the plastic pumps can be hard to recycle because they have springs inside.

YOUR 2-MINUTE MISSION: **Change your soap! Get rid of the liquid stuff and replace it with a bar of solid soap that comes wrapped in paper.**
10 POINTS

Shampoo, conditioner, and shower gel come in single-use plastic bottles. While they can be recycled, it's better to do without.

YOUR 2-MINUTE MISSION: **Try out a solid shampoo bar and use solid soap instead of shower gel.**
10 POINTS

Toilet paper isn't made of plastic but often comes wrapped in plastic.

> YOUR 2-MINUTE MISSION: **At your local supermarket, try to find toilet paper that comes wrapped in paper.**
> **10 POINTS**

Cotton swabs often have plastic sticks.

> YOUR 2-MINUTE MISSION: **Look for cotton swabs with paper sticks. Buy these instead, or consider whether you can do without.**
> **10 POINTS**

★ EVERYDAY SUPERHERO ★

Name: Rowena

Job: Makeup designer

Superpower: Makes waste-free products

How she fights plastic: Creates soaps and shampoos that don't come in bottles

Top tip: Shampoo bars last a long time and produce no plastic waste

Hates: Things not getting reused

Loves: Living on a clean, tidy planet

ROWENA

MISSION 10

FIGHT PLASTIC IN YOUR TOILET

Who's up for a visit to the sewage plant? Bring a clothespin. It might get stinky. This is where all your pee and poop goes after you flush the toilet. Sadly, it's where lots of other stuff ends up too. And that's a problem for the ocean.

THINK BEFORE YOU FLUSH

Whenever you flush your toilet, everything in the toilet bowl goes down your pipes, into the sewers, and down to the sewage-treatment plant, where it gets filtered and cleaned.

The trouble is that the filters at the sewage plants can't catch everything. Small things, like cotton-swab sticks, escape and make their way through the water system and out to sea. Wet wipes—which are made of plastic—get caught up in the sewage system or in fatbergs, which are giant lumps of congealed fat that form from grease and oil that have been poured down people's sinks.

WHEN THINGS GET SMELLY

When extremely heavy rain means there is too much water for the sewage system to process, water companies relieve the pressure by releasing raw sewage through huge pipes called combined sewer overflows (CSOs). All the pee, poop, puke, and paper and anything else that's been flushed goes straight out to sea and can eventually end up on the beach. That means all the bandages, cotton swabs, wet wipes, and tampon applicators end up on MY BEACH. We pick them up all the time, and it is horrible!

YOUR 2-MINUTE MISSION: **Ask your teacher to organize a visit to your local sewage-treatment plant. It might not sound like fun, but it'll be VERY interesting.**
100 POINTS

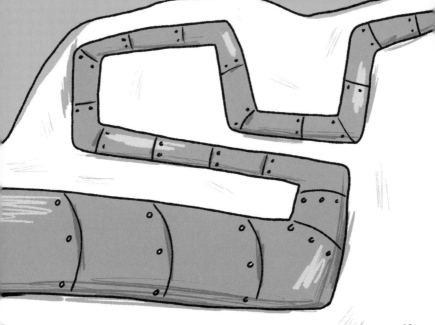

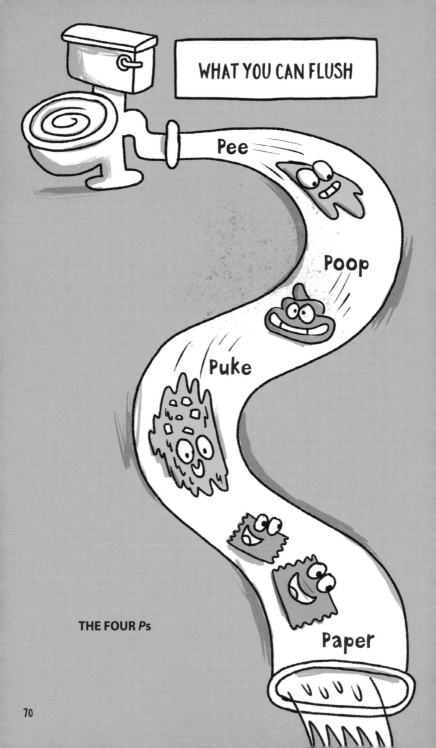

WHAT YOU CAN FLUSH

Pee

Poop

Puke

Paper

THE FOUR *P*s

WHAT YOU CAN'T FLUSH

Cotton-swab
sticks

Wet wipes

Glitter

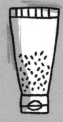

Microbeads

Toy soldiers

Plastic bags

Tampons

Bandages

Cotton pads

Gauze

**ANYTHING
THAT'S NOT
ONE OF THE
FOUR *P*s**

LOVE YOUR TOILET

Remember that only pee, paper, puke, and poop can go down the toilet!

YOUR 2-MINUTE MISSION: Count the number of toilets that you use regularly. Make a sign for each one that says: ONLY PEE, PAPER, PUKE, AND POOP DOWN THIS TOILET—THANK YOU!
20 POINTS

Find out from your family what they flush down the toilet.

YOUR 2-MINUTE MISSION: If your family flushes anything down the toilet that isn't one of the Four *P*s, ask if you can put a wastebasket—with a lid—next to the toilet, for everything else. These items can then go in the trash or be recycled.
20 POINTS

FACTBERG: In 2018, a fatberg—a lump of wet wipes, grease, and oils from kitchen waste—210 feet (64 meters) long was found in the sewers of Devon, England. That's longer than four and a half city buses!

Wet wipes are often made from plastic and should never be flushed. We find lots of them on beach cleans. The thing is, a washcloth will do the job just as well, and it can be reused!

YOUR 2-MINUTE MISSION: **If your family uses wet wipes, make a sign for your toilet reminding everyone not to flush them! Better yet, switch to reusable cloth. 10 POINTS**

EVERYDAY SUPERHERO

Name: Shayna

Job: Flesh-footed shearwater

Superpower: Dodging fishermen

How she fights plastic: Appeared on TV with a stomach full of plastic

Top tip: DON'T FLUSH IT! Plastic looks and tastes like food to seabirds.

Hates: Being made to throw up to get rid of plastic

Loves: Being rescued and not having a stomach full of plastic

SHAYNA

FIGHT PLASTIC IN YOUR CLOSET

I know what you're thinking! You're thinking that there's no plastic in your closet, aren't you? Believe it or not, your closet—or bedroom floor, if that's where you keep your clothes—is a good place to fight plastic. Lots of clothes are made from synthetic fibers that are plastic, including nylon, Lycra, and polyester. And when they are washed, plastic clothes shed lots of tiny fibers, called microfibers, that go down drains to the ocean.

WHY PLASTIC IS THE NEW OLD

Nylon, polyester, acrylic, and other synthetic fibers (that don't come from nature) are all made from different types of polymers (plastics) and won't break down or biodegrade. Athletic shirts, school uniforms, sports socks, and outdoor jackets are often made from synthetic fibers. You can easily check what materials have been used by looking at the labels.

It's the same with sparkly stuff like sequins. Sadly, they are made from plastic and are very difficult to recycle. Fake fur trims on coats are also made from synthetic fibers.

You can avoid plastic in your clothes by choosing natural alternatives, like wool, cotton, hemp, silk, or bamboo.

FASHION FACTS

A British study showed that most items in the average closet are often worn just seven times before being thrown away!

Another study showed that every person, on average, has fifty-seven unworn items in their wardrobe.

Synthetic fibers are almost always made from plastic.

Synthetic fibers are non-biodegradable, which means they will never go away.

Most materials used in the fashion industry are made of synthetic fibers.

WHY WASHING CLOTHES IS BAD FOR YOU

Microfibers are tiny plastic fibers that come off your clothes when you wash them. They are one of the biggest sources of plastic in the ocean. Imagine the fluff in your dryer going down the drain each time you wash your clothes! Eek. Sewage-treatment plants are unable to catch these fibers, so they go straight into a river or the ocean. The fibers don't break down and instead are eaten by plankton and tiny fish. If those fish are eaten by bigger fish, the fibers move up the food chain and can potentially be eaten by us. Yuck!

THE GOOD: NATURAL FIBERS

Jeans made of cotton

Sweaters made of wool

Hawaiian shirts made of rayon

Undies made of bamboo

EVERYDAY SUPERHERO

Name: Linda

Job: Fashion designer

Superpower: Turns garbage into beautiful clothes

How she fights plastic: Creates dresses made from ocean plastic

Top tip: Don't look the other way!

Hates: Companies pretending to be green to sell more products

Loves: Fighting plastic together

LINDA

THE BAD: SYNTHETIC FIBERS

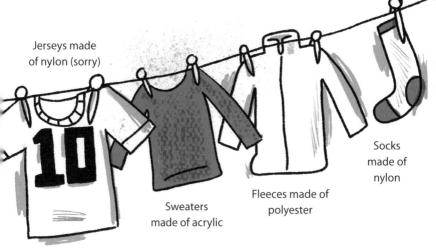

Jerseys made of nylon (sorry)

Sweaters made of acrylic

Fleeces made of polyester

Socks made of nylon

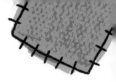

HOW TO FIGHT PLASTIC IN YOUR CLOSET

The secret to fighting plastic in your closet is to choose your clothes carefully and make them last by loving them for as long as you can before buying new ones. Here are some other ideas:

1. Learn how to sew! Sewing up holes will keep your clothes from wearing out, which means you'll be able to wear them again and again and again.

> **YOUR 2-MINUTE MISSION: Learn how to sew up holes in your old clothes.**
> **10 POINTS**

2. Wash your nylon, polyester, and synthetic-fiber clothes less often. Less often means less plastic goes in the sea.

> **YOUR 2-MINUTE MISSION: Separate your clothes that are made of synthetic fibers from those made of natural fibers. Wash them less often.**
> **10 POINTS**

3. Wash your synthetic-fiber clothes in a special bag or with a ball that will catch the microfibers before they enter the water system.

> **YOUR 2-MINUTE MISSION:** **Catch microfibers in the washing machine with a specially designed bag or ball. Throw out the fibers.**
> **10 POINTS**

4. Pass your old clothes on to a friend or relative, or send your old clothes to a charity store or yard sale. Just don't throw them out! (And shop at thrift stores when you can!)

> **YOUR 2-MINUTE MISSION:** **Organize a clothes swap at school or at a club. Bring in the clothes you don't love anymore and swap them for your friends' unloved clothes.**
> **10 POINTS**

5. Get creative and try upcycling! Jazz up your old clothes with plastic-free dyes, fabric paint, and extra decorations.

> **YOUR 2-MINUTE MISSION:** **Make yourself your very own #2minutesuperhero costume out of your old clothes.**
> **20 POINTS**

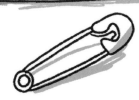

FIGHT PLASTIC ON THE FIELD, COURT, AND TRACK

Sports are great! But plastic on the field is awful! As soon as it rains, any post-game litter could get washed down a drain, into a river, and then out to sea. It's going to take a superhero to tackle the problem.

PLASTIC-FREE GAMES

Sporting legends need hydration and sustenance. And that means you! You need water and snacks on the field, whether you are playing hockey, running cross-country, biking, swimming, or kicking a ball around in the park. But remember to make sure your snacks and water are plastic-free!

RUNNING SCARES: At the Boston Marathon, around 62,000 single-use plastic bottles and 1.4 million water cups are used.

YOUR 2-MINUTE MISSION:
Declare your sports events plastic-free. If you take snacks, opt for fruit or homemade granola bars, and ALWAYS remember to carry your reusable water bottle! **20 POINTS**

CLEAR UP BEFORE AND AFTER KICKOFF

Doing a **#2minutelitterpick** before you start your game will ensure your field is clean and safe. Then do it again afterward, and leave your field or track nicer than it was when you arrived. If you do this when you go to play at other schools, they will be VERY impressed. You'll be showing them what to do!

YOUR 2-MINUTE MISSION: Get your team to do a litter pick after every game. Take a bag and pick up any litter. Recycle what you can. You will look great and will be WINNING, no matter what the score is.
30 POINTS

EVERYDAY SUPERHERO

Name: Pete

Job: Cleans beaches

Superpower: Never giving up. Not ever. Not even when it seems impossible.

How he fights plastic: Leads a group of happy beach and street cleaners

Top tip: Being outside makes you happier. Walking on a clean beach is a very happy thing.

Hates: Gross juice from trash cans

Loves: Gadgets to put on his gadget belt

PETE

GO PLOGGING!

Plogging is a Scandinavian idea where joggers pick up litter as they run. It's very simple—you just run and pick up litter! Do it during the warm-up!

YOUR 2-MINUTE MISSION:
Grab a bag at lunchtime and go plogging around the playground!
30 POINTS

FIGHT PLASTIC ON THE WEEKEND

Now that you've got the superhero bug, your weekends and vacations are going to be completely different! You'll see the world through new eyes and find yourself spotting trash, avoiding single-use plastic, and making sure you leave places you go nicer than they were when you got there. What a fantastic thing! You are a #2minutesuperhero, making the world better wherever you go!

PLASTIC-FREE DAYS OUT

Going to the beach? Yay! Join me in a **#2minutebeachclean**. It's easy. Set a timer, grab a bag, and GO! How much plastic can you find? And if you're having ice cream afterward, treat yourself to a cone—for plastic-free licking!

YOUR 2-MINUTE MISSION: **Do a #2minutebeachclean and see what you find. Look for plastic bags, bottles, bottle tops, cotton-swab sticks, wet wipes, and pieces of fishing net. They are the most common items we find. But also look for Lego bricks, toy soldiers, fishing lines, and old flip-flops.**
10 POINTS

FIGHT PLASTIC AT THE THEATER

Off to the movies? Take a paper straw and perhaps even your own reusable cup! Popcorn, of course, often comes in paper or cardboard, so you're good to go. Just watch out for the bags of candy and plastic cutlery. Take your trash home instead of leaving it—then you can recycle it!

> **YOUR 2-MINUTE MISSION:**
> **Make it a plastic-free movie night!**
> **10 POINTS**

FIGHT PLASTIC AT THE THEME PARK

Going to a theme park? It can be a challenge! But you can do it. Take sandwiches, your reusable water bottle, and your own homemade snacks to enjoy a plastic-free day of amusements. Say no to plastic straws or bring your own paper one.

MAKING FAST FOOD PLASTIC-FREE

Fast food doesn't have to be plastic food. Refuse plastic straws and cutlery, choose cups without lids, and say no to those horrible plastic sauce packets.

FAST FUTURES? There is a growing movement to ban plastic straws. So perhaps you'll have a lower-plastic—and happier—meal soon!

SLEEP WELL ON YOUR SLEEPOVERS

Going to stay at other people's houses for parties and sleepovers doesn't mean you can't be plastic-free. Remember your reusable water bottle and pack reusable cutlery. Sweet dreams!

EVERYDAY SUPERHERO

Name: The Super Whale

Job: Humpback whale

Superpower: Sings songs that can be heard for hundreds of miles

How she fights plastic: Battled a plastic fishing net twice—and won!—with help from British Divers Marine Life Rescue

Top tip: Don't swim near nets

Hates: Being tangled up in rope

Loves: Swimming in a clean ocean

THE SUPER WHALE

FIGHT PLASTIC WITH YOUR ALLOWANCE

If you're anything like the average superhero, you get a whopping $454 in allowance each year. That's an average of $8.74 a week. And you save about 43 percent of it.

That means you spend some of it. And that's important. How you spend your money is vital in the fight against plastic. You can vote for a better world by making smart buying choices.

SUPERHERO SPENDING

If you play your cards right, you could even get money for being a superhero! How? You might earn money for doing chores, such as cleaning the kitchen and bathroom, helping with the shopping, or even doing the gardening. As part of your superhero training, you'll be doing all those things anyway! So why not use your superhero training to boost your earnings?

89

SHOW THE WORLD BY BUYING WELL

What do you normally spend your money on? How you spend your allowance is your chance to show everyone what you want the world to be like. You can send a strong message to companies by choosing not to buy toys or candy that are wrapped in plastic or made from plastic (the toys, not the candy!). Also, don't buy comics and magazines that are wrapped in plastic or come with plastic toys. You don't want things that are likely to break or be quickly discarded.

YOUR 2-MINUTE MISSION: Stop spending your money on one item that contains plastic. If it's candy, buy in bulk instead. If it's toys, buy something that is plastic-free and you will keep.
20 POINTS

BUYING PLASTIC-FREE CANDY

You don't have to buy candy wrapped in plastic. Take a trip to a bulk shop where they sell candy individually. Just beware of plastic packaging. You could even take your own bags or containers!

BUYING TOYS FOR LIFE

Lots of toys are made of plastic. The secret here is to buy toys that you will use for a long time—and can then sell or give away later. So that means buying carefully, perhaps saving for something more expensive, and finding things that won't break easily and that you know you'll play with a lot.

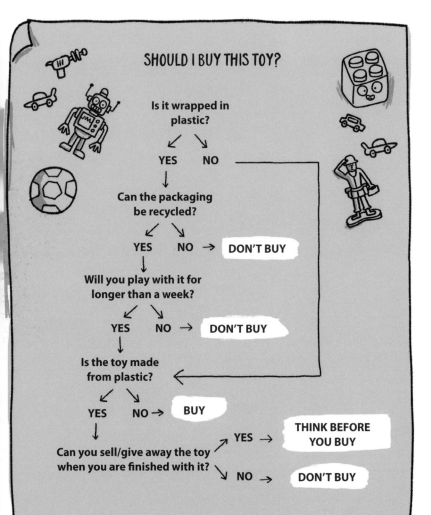

SHOULD I BUY THIS TOY?

Is it wrapped in plastic?

YES → Can the packaging be recycled?

NO →

Can the packaging be recycled?

YES → Will you play with it for longer than a week?

NO → **DON'T BUY**

Will you play with it for longer than a week?

YES → Is the toy made from plastic?

NO → **DON'T BUY**

Is the toy made from plastic?

YES → Can you sell/give away the toy when you are finished with it?

NO → **BUY**

Can you sell/give away the toy when you are finished with it?

YES → **THINK BEFORE YOU BUY**

NO → **DON'T BUY**

EARN MONEY FROM YOUR OLD STUFF

You can make money by selling toys, clothes, games, and books that you no longer need or want. This also means that you can make sure your stuff goes to a good home and will be reused. Throwing things away just because you are finished with them is a shame—especially when someone else might love them.

With help from an adult, visit sites like eBay or Craigslist, which are great for selling old toys, books, and games. You could also organize a yard sale. Get your family to help you.

WHAT TO DO WITH YOUR OLD STUFF

CLOTHES

- Sell
- Donate to stores that will reuse or recycle your used stuff and give you a discount in exchange
- Give to charity

BOOKS

- Sell
- Give to relatives or friends
- Donate to library book sales

TOYS

- Sell
- Give to relatives or friends
- Donate to children's charities or toy libraries

YOUR 2-MINUTE MISSION: **Ask your school to organize a yard sale, where you and your friends can sell your unwanted books, toys, and clothes—and earn money too!**
40 POINTS

FIGHT PLASTIC BY FIXING IT

If one of your toys breaks, fix it! It's pretty simple. Don't just throw it away. Nowadays there are places called repair cafés where you can get your old stuff fixed so you can keep using it. This is great because it means you don't have to buy something new, and you can keep loving your old stuff for longer.

FIGHT PLASTIC IN YOUR CELEBRATIONS

Holidays and birthdays are often filled with food, family, and fun. I love them! But sadly, many of these celebration days have become all-out plastic fests of wastefulness. If you want to fight plastic, you're going to have to rethink how you celebrate. The good news, though? You don't have to give up the treats.

NO MORE PLASTIC WRAPPING

Lots of foil-backed and shiny wrapping paper is plastic. You can tell by scrunching it up. If it stays scrunched, it's paper. If it expands again, it's plastic. Go for the paper wrapping, and you'll be able to recycle or reuse it later.

WRAP UP THE WASTE: An estimated 330 million square feet (31 million square meters) of wrapping paper gets sent to landfills each year.

FIGHT PLASTIC WITH YOUR PRESENTS

The giving of gifts is a symbolic gesture. So save your money and make a homemade gift instead of buying something made of plastic or packaged in plastic. Make cookies or other treats instead. Give a gift with love—the ocean will thank you.

YOUR 2-MINUTE MISSION: **Make presents for your family and wrap them in paper, newspaper, or paper you have decorated yourself. Tie them up with string, since tape is plastic!**
30 POINTS

DECORATIONS

Whether you're decorating a Christmas tree or festooning the house with hearts for Valentine's Day, there are amazing alternatives to tinsel, ornaments, and glittery decorations, which are all made of plastic. Try hanging popcorn chains, paper hearts, or other fun homemade options.

WASTEFUL FACT: Between Thanksgiving and New Year's, Americans generate an additional 1 million tons (about 900,000 metric tons) of household waste.

A CHRISTMAS TREE FOREVER

Each year, millions of trees are cut down for Christmas. What a waste! If you want an artificial tree, buy it secondhand and reuse it every year. But if you can, buy a locally grown Christmas tree in a pot that you can bring inside and decorate each year. Better still, make your own tree out of driftwood or sticks.

FEEL THE LOVE

Valentine's Day is a great time to show people you care about them, but there's no need to do it with plastic! Rather than exchanging plastic toys or glittery items, stick to traditional valentines made of paper.

YOUR 2-MINUTE MISSION: **Make paper chains for decorations. You can use different colors for all the holidays.**
10 POINTS

THE FIGHT-PLASTIC FESTIVITIES

Say no to:

- 🌲 Plastic ornaments
- 🌲 Glittery decorations
- 🌲 Plastic and foil wrapping paper
- 🌲 Tape
- 🌲 Gift bags
- 🌲 Store-bought cards (especially ones with glitter)
- 🌲 Plastic packaging
- 🌲 Plastic straws
- 🌲 Plastic cups, plates, and cutlery

LOVE A PLASTIC-FREE CELEBRATION

Feel the festive joy with:

- 🌲 Paper chains made from old magazines and newspapers
- 🌲 Homemade decorations
- 🌲 Homemade cards
- 🌲 Gifts tied with string
- 🌲 Wrapping paper made from newsprint or brown paper
- 🌲 Home-baked goods

THE SCARY THING ABOUT HALLOWEEN?

It's not the ghouls. It's the plastic! Waste companies hate Halloween. There's just so much waste from discarded costumes, plastic skulls, and scary decorations. So how about making a costume out of old clothes this year? I bet there are some horrors in your parents' closet that you could use! For trick-or-treating, fill a bowl with chocolates and sweets that come in paper and foil wrappers instead of plastic. EASY!

THE FRIGHTENING TRUTH: It is estimated that around 35 million Halloween costumes are purchased each year in the US. That's a lot of material destined for the landfill!

YOUR 2-MINUTE MISSION: Make a Halloween costume out of things you wear every day. Or borrow something silly. A scary hairstyle or face paint can transform an outfit into something really terrifying. Make it your mission to have a plastic-free Halloween. **20 POINTS**

A PLASTIC-FREE SPRING

Spring should be a time to celebrate new life and the beauty of the planet. But for those who celebrate with Easter baskets, it can mean lots of plastic waste.

Let me out!

OUT WITH THE PLASTIC!

Special holiday treats like Easter eggs are often overpackaged, with plastic inserts holding them in place. But some aren't! Look for treats wrapped in cardboard and tinfoil. Both are 100 percent recyclable.

EGGSTRA WASTE: More than 250 million plastic Easter eggs are sold each year in the US.

YOUR 2-MINUTE MISSION: Make sure the chocolate and other holiday sweets you eat are not covered in plastic. Choose your treats wisely!
10 POINTS

THE FIGHT-PLASTIC PARTY!

It's time to celebrate. You're nearly at the end of your plastic-fighting odyssey, and your superhero status awaits. So it's time to PARTY! I like plastic-free parties where there is no waste. Other than things to recycle, there's nothing left afterward except good memories, sleepy eyes, and exhausted dancing feet. Are you ready? It's the Fight-Plastic Party for all the #2minutesuperheroes!

YOUR 2-MINUTE MISSION: Next time you have a birthday party or celebration, make it a FIGHT-PLASTIC PARTY! Plan carefully. Make your own decorations and cook up a party-food fiesta! Use the lists in this mission to help you.
150 POINTS

THE EVIL PARTY VILLAINS

- **Balloons:** Sadly, you're going to have to pop your balloon habit. Balloons, even those that claim to be biodegradable, are a menace to wildlife.

- **Glitter:** Glitter is fun. But the minute it goes down the drain, it becomes a dangerous microplastic that washes straight into the sea.

- **Goody bags:** You must resist the plastic goody bag. Avoid plastic toys and individually wrapped sweets and snacks such as lollipops.

- **Party food:** So much party food comes in plastic packaging. From frozen pizza to store-bought cupcakes, supermarkets seem to give you more plastic than party. Fight back!

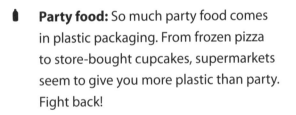

- **Plastic plates and cutlery:** No, no, no, no, no! Plastic plates, knives, forks, and spoons may be recyclable, but it is better to do without.

- **Straws:** Always say no to plastic straws. Instead use paper straws . . . or no straws at all!

BUBBLE-BURSTING FACT: To sea turtles, balloons and plastic bags look just like jellyfish—their favorite food.

EVERYDAY SUPERHERO

Name: Bob

Job: Green turtle

Superpower: Swims more than 1,500 miles (2,400 kilometers) to nest and breed

How he fights plastic: Was rescued and then made to poop out all the balloons and plastic bags he'd eaten

Top tip: Don't let go of balloons! Even the biodegradable ones can be harmful.

Hates: That balloons look like food

Loves: Delicious seagrasses

BOB

THE GOOD GUYS

- **Homemade decorations:** Paper chains and lanterns are easy and fun to make. And the best thing? You can reuse and recycle them!

- **Bunting:** Paper bunting made from string and colored paper or magazines is cool. You can also sew some from old material and ribbon!

- **Paper table decorations:** Newsprint paper—which you can buy in rolls at hobby shops—is great for using as tablecloths and wrapping paper. Put crayons on the tables and invite your friends to decorate it!

- **Paper party bags:** Use brown paper bags and plastic-free party favors such as notebooks, masks, and pencils.

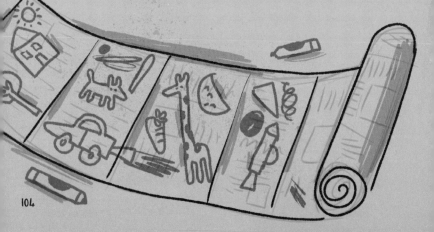

- **Real party food:** It's easy to avoid plastic-wrapped party food. But you might have to work at it. Make your own sandwiches, muffins, brownies, and cakes!

- **Plates and cutlery:** You don't need plastic plates when you could use real plates and wash them afterward. If you need more, borrow them from friends.

- **Straws:** You don't have to party without straws! You can buy paper straws from the supermarket if you want them.

EVERYDAY SUPERHERO

Name: Dolly

Job: Online campaigner

Superpower: Technology

How she fights plastic: Running online campaigns to keep people from releasing balloons and buying plastic

Top tip: Buy less, use less, and reuse stuff more

Hates: Balloons

Loves: Picnics on the beach

DOLLY

FIGHT PLASTIC WITH YOUR VOICE

Congratulations on completing the #2minutesuperhero training! But there is one final mission before you're done. It's very simple and can make a huge difference because it will let the people in power know what you think about plastic.

YOUR 2-MINUTE MISSION: **Write a letter or an email to someone who is responsible for making decisions that affect your fight against plastic. It could be a congressperson, a city councillor, a teacher, or your principal. Tell them what worries you about plastic, what you need them to do, and why. Use the template on the next page to get started. Go for it! Your voice matters.**

100 POINTS

Find your representatives here:
www.commoncause.org/find-your-representative

Dear [Name],

My name is [add your name] and I am [your age] years old. I attend [name your school here], and I am writing to you about plastic.

I am very worried about the health of our oceans and I am also worried about my future due to the overuse, production, and bad management of plastic. I believe that we have to do all we can to keep plastic from entering the oceans by recycling more, stopping plastic at the source, and using less of it in our daily lives.

I have taken a pledge to fight plastic, and I now want you to do your part to help. I want you to fine companies that pollute the oceans. I need you to support laws to keep companies from giving the public unnecessary plastic and to encourage companies to use recycled plastic in all their products.

We also need an immediate ban on ALL single-use plastics and a simple recycling system that is the same for everyone, wherever you live. We need it now.

Can you do this for me and my future? I hope so. Please reply with your pledge against plastic.

Yours,
[Sign your name here]

MISSION COMPLETED

Close your eyes . . .
Imagine standing on a spotless beach, staring out at a vast ocean that is free of plastic and pulsing with life, surf, and wonder. Whales are blowing waterspouts, and dolphins are spinning. Flying fish skim across the sunlit surface of the water. Beneath the waves, fish and seals are dancing. Above you, seagulls squawk and squabble.

You can smell the fresh air and the seaweed, feel the wind on your skin, taste the salt on your lips, and hear the crashing of the waves.

The ocean is beautiful, and you are a part of it, wherever you live. A turtle pops up just in front of you, surprising you a little. It smiles and says, "Thank you!"

You did that.
How does it feel?
YOU ARE A #2MINUTESUPERHERO.
MISSION COMPLETED.

YOUR SUPERHERO RATING

SUPERHERO POINTS

Now that you've finished your training, it's time to find out what kind of superhero you are. Add up the points you've earned after completing your missions.

MISSION 1: GET TO KNOW THE BAD STUFF

Find five pieces of good plastic that you use every day.
10 POINTS

Find five pieces of bad plastic that will be used only once before being thrown away.
20 POINTS

TOTAL POSSIBLE MISSION POINTS: 30

MISSION 2: FIGHT PLASTIC IN YOUR TRASH CAN

Get a food-waste bin and start a compost heap! Find out how to make compost in Mission 8.
30 POINTS

Make a trash chart and mark it each time anyone takes out the trash. Monitor how many trash bags your family puts out each week and see if you can cut it in half.
50 POINTS

Visit a materials recovery facility (MRF) near you.
50 POINTS

Find three straws—one that is plastic, one that is biodegradable plastic, and one that is paper. Get a plant pot and fill it with mud. Then poke the straws halfway into the mud. Leave them for a couple of weeks and see what happens!

20 POINTS

TOTAL POSSIBLE MISSION POINTS: 150

MISSION 3: FIGHT PLASTIC IN YOUR PARK

Do a **#2minutelitterpick**. On your walk home from school or at the park, spend two minutes filling an old tote bag with litter. Recycle what you can, and trash the rest. How much did you get in two minutes?

20 POINTS

TOTAL POSSIBLE MISSION POINTS: 20

MISSION 4: FIGHT PLASTIC IN YOUR BACKPACK

Have a pen amnesty! Ask all your friends to empty their schoolbags and collect their old pens. Then ask a teacher or parent to help you raise money for a zero-waste box at **www.terracycle.com**. You can send your pens to them for recycling.

80 POINTS

Does your school have a water fountain where you can fill your water bottle? Fill up! If not, how about starting a petition for a fountain or bottle-refilling station at school? You could ask your parents and your friends' parents to sign it too!

30 POINTS

Sadly, if it comes wrapped in plastic, it may be time to stop buying your old candy. But it's also time to go candy shopping. Get yourself some mints in a tin! Look for candy sold in cardboard!

10 POINTS

Collect all your chip bags. Collect all your friends' bags. With help from a parent or teacher, set up a chip-bag recycling point and raise money for a zero-waste box. Send the bags off to be recycled. Find out more at **www.terracycle.com**.

80 POINTS

TOTAL POSSIBLE MISSION POINTS: 200

MISSION 5: FIGHT PLASTIC IN YOUR LUNCHROOM

At your next lunch break, ask three friends to show you their lunches. Show them yours. Do your lunches contain plastic? Make a vow to cut out AT LEAST one piece of plastic from lunch.

10 POINTS

Show and tell! Ask your teacher if you can talk to your class or in assembly about your **#2minutesuperhero** mission. Explain why you are trying to reduce plastic and how you are doing it. Ask your fellow students to sign a pledge to help you.

50 POINTS

Does your school have a recycling point for single-use plastics such as yogurt containers, straws, and bottles? If not, set one up! Get

permission from your teacher and principal. Make labels so everyone can see what goes where.

40 POINTS

TOTAL POSSIBLE MISSION POINTS: 100

MISSION 6: FIGHT PLASTIC IN THE SUPERMARKET

Offer to help with the shopping so that you'll be able to have a say in the food you buy as a family.

20 POINTS

Go on a plastic-free shopping trip and come back with ZERO waste!

40 POINTS

TOTAL POSSIBLE MISSION POINTS: 60

MISSION 7: FIGHT PLASTIC IN YOUR KITCHEN

Become the bag police! Announce a zero-tolerance plastic grocery-bag policy. Make sure every member of your family has NO EXCUSE for using a plastic bag. Put canvas bags in the car, under the sink, and always close by, then charge each family member 10¢ for every plastic grocery bag they use.

20 POINTS

Trade plastic scrubbers for coconut-husk or metal ones and refill your dish-soap bottle at a store that sells in bulk.

30 POINTS

Choose your favorite cereal. Find the biggest and smallest boxes of it that you can. Figure out how many bowls of cereal each box contains and how many boxes of each size you'd need to fill one hundred bowls.

10 POINTS

Make beeswax wraps with an adult. Find your brightest cotton fabric and paint it with beeswax (buy it online). If you are vegan, use plant-based wax. You can add pine resin to make the wraps sticky.

40 POINTS

TOTAL POSSIBLE MISSION POINTS: 100

MISSION 8: FIGHT PLASTIC IN YOUR GARDEN

Use the compost you made in Mission 2. Put some compost into pots and plant some sunflower seeds. Watch them grow really tall!

20 POINTS

Cut a clear plastic bottle in half and fill the bottom with compost. Insert three pea seeds into the compost around the bottle's edge. Water and leave on a windowsill. You'll be able to see the seeds germinate and the seedlings grow. When they're big enough, plant them outside in a larger pot. Enjoy fresh pea shoots in your salad or wait to eat the peas.

20 POINTS

Talk to your teacher about starting a gardening club or growing vegetables in your classroom. Bring in leftover plastic pots, trays, and containers, and then take the vegetables home when they're big enough to eat.

20 POINTS

TOTAL POSSIBLE MISSION POINTS: 60

MISSION 9: FIGHT PLASTIC IN YOUR BATHROOM

Try a toothbrush made of bamboo, one of the world's fastest-growing and most sustainable materials. When it's time to replace it, you can put it in your compost.

20 POINTS

Try toothpaste that comes in a glass jar or in tablet form. It might not be what you are used to, but it will work and is a great way to fight plastic twice a day!

20 POINTS

Change your soap! Get rid of the liquid stuff and replace it with a bar of solid soap that comes wrapped in paper.

10 POINTS

Try out a solid shampoo bar and use solid soap instead of shower gel.

10 POINTS

At your local supermarket, try to find toilet paper that comes wrapped in paper.

10 POINTS

Look for cotton swabs with paper sticks. Buy these instead, or consider whether you can do without.

10 POINTS

TOTAL POSSIBLE MISSION POINTS: 80

MISSION 10: FIGHT PLASTIC IN YOUR TOILET

Ask your teacher to organize a visit to your local sewage-treatment plant. It might not sound like fun, but it'll be VERY interesting.

100 POINTS

Count the number of toilets that you use regularly. Make a sign for each one that says: ONLY PEE, PAPER, PUKE, AND POOP DOWN THIS TOILET—THANK YOU!

20 POINTS

If your family flushes anything down the toilet that isn't one of the Four *P*s, ask if you can put a wastebasket—with a lid—next to the toilet, for everything else. These items can then go in the trash or be recycled.

20 POINTS

If your family uses wet wipes, make a sign for your toilet reminding everyone not to flush them! Better yet, switch to reusable cloth.

10 POINTS

TOTAL POSSIBLE MISSION POINTS: 150

MISSION II: FIGHT PLASTIC IN YOUR CLOSET

Learn how to sew up holes in your old clothes.

10 POINTS

Separate your clothes that are made of synthetic fibers from those made of natural fibers. Wash them less often.

10 POINTS

Catch microfibers in the washing machine with a specially designed bag or ball. Throw out the fibers.

10 POINTS

Organize a clothes swap at school or at a club. Bring in the clothes you don't love anymore and swap them for your friends' unloved clothes.

10 POINTS

Make yourself your very own **#2minutesuperhero** costume out of your old clothes.

20 POINTS

TOTAL POSSIBLE MISSION POINTS: 60

MISSION 12: FIGHT PLASTIC ON THE FIELD, COURT, AND TRACK

Declare your sports events plastic-free. If you take snacks, opt for fruit or homemade granola bars, and ALWAYS remember to carry your reusable water bottle!

20 POINTS

Get your team to do a litter pick after every game. Take a bag and pick up any litter. Recycle what you can. You will look great and will be WINNING, no matter what the score is.

30 POINTS

Grab a bag at lunchtime and go plogging around the playground!

30 POINTS

TOTAL POSSIBLE MISSION POINTS: 80

MISSION 13: FIGHT PLASTIC ON THE WEEKEND

Do a **#2minutebeachclean** and see what you find. Look for plastic bags, bottles, bottle tops, cotton-swab sticks, wet wipes, and pieces of fishing net. They are the most common items we find. But also look for Lego bricks, toy soldiers, fishing lines, and old flip-flops.

10 POINTS

Make it a plastic-free movie night!

10 POINTS

Go to your favorite fast-food restaurant and test them to see if you can make your fast food a plastic-free affair. You can!

10 POINTS

TOTAL POSSIBLE MISSION POINTS: 30

MISSION 14: FIGHT PLASTIC WITH YOUR ALLOWANCE

Stop spending your money on one item that contains plastic. If it's candy, buy in bulk. If it's toys, buy something that is plastic-free and you will keep.

20 POINTS

Ask your school to organize a yard sale, where you and your friends can sell your unwanted books, toys, and clothes—and earn money too!

40 POINTS

TOTAL POSSIBLE MISSION POINTS: 60

MISSION 15: FIGHT PLASTIC IN YOUR CELEBRATIONS

Make presents for your family and wrap them in paper, newspaper, or paper you have decorated yourself. Tie them up with string, since tape is plastic!

30 POINTS

Make paper chains for decorations. You can use different colors for all the holidays.

10 POINTS

Make a Halloween costume out of things you wear every day. Or borrow something silly. A scary hairstyle or face paint can transform an outfit into something really terrifying. Make it your mission to have a plastic-free Halloween.

20 POINTS

Make sure the chocolate and other holiday sweets you eat are not covered in plastic. Choose your treats wisely!

10 POINTS

TOTAL POSSIBLE MISSION POINTS: 70

MISSION 16: THE FIGHT-PLASTIC PARTY

Next time you have a birthday party or celebration, make it a FIGHT-PLASTIC PARTY! Plan carefully. Make your own decorations and cook up a party-food fiesta! Use the lists in this mission to help you.

150 POINTS

TOTAL POSSIBLE MISSION POINTS: 150

BONUS MISSION: FIGHT PLASTIC WITH YOUR VOICE

Write a letter or an email to someone who is responsible for making decisions that affect your fight against plastic. It could be a congressperson, a city councillor, a teacher, or your principal. Tell them what worries you about plastic, what you need them to do, and why. Go for it! Your voice matters.

100 POINTS

TOTAL POSSIBLE MISSION POINTS: 100

WHAT KIND OF SUPERHERO ARE YOU?

Now that you've completed the two-minute missions, add up your points. What kind of #2minutesuperhero are you?

0–499 POINTS

You are my kind of superhero. You are getting there, putting in the effort, trying hard. And that's what matters. You have completed enough missions to start making a real difference. You care. You try to influence others. You are using your voice to make changes to your world.

Now is the time to make the most of your progress and do even more to save the oceans. So put on your cape and mask and go out into the world to do even more for the planet. Everything you do makes a difference!

MISSION COMPLETE: You're a 3 ★ Superhero

500–999 POINTS

You have a whole superhero thing going on! You have completed most of the missions, and that makes you a super-duper superhero. You have shown a real commitment to the oceans and a love of all things wild. The dolphins, whales, and fish thank you.

What next? Complete the remaining missions and give the oceans one last push for their future. You can do it. You got this far by being a caring, plastic-fighting warrior! You can go the whole way. GO, YOU!

MISSION COMPLETE: You are a 4 ★ Superhero

1,000—1,500 POINTS

Oh, my word! You are the Hero of Superheroes. How will you sleep at night with all the praise I am about to give you? You have truly embraced the fight-plastic spirit and channeled your inner everyday superhero. Without a doubt, you have single-handedly saved dolphins, seals, whales, and birds from plastic. Your work matters, and all your actions, combined with the actions of all the other superheroes out there, have made a real difference.

Thank you and well done.

MISSION COMPLETE: You get the 5 ★ Superhero Award

IMAGINE YOUR PHOTO HERE

EVERYDAY SUPERHERO

What's your name?

What's your job?

What's your superpower?

How do you fight plastic?

What's your top tip?

What do you hate?

What do you love?

YOU

FIND OUT MORE ABOUT THE FIGHT AGAINST PLASTIC

Want to learn more? Excellent! Take a look at these:

Greenpeace: A global organization that defends the natural world and is campaigning to stop the flow of plastic into the ocean
www.greenpeace.org/usa/oceans/preventing-plastic-pollution

National Geographic Kids: A kids' magazine that includes tips for reducing plastic use
www.kids.nationalgeographic.com/explore/nature/kids-vs -plastic

Ocean Conservancy: A foundation dedicated to protecting the ocean
www.oceanconservancy.org/trash-free-seas

Plastic Oceans: A nonprofit organization dedicated to ending plastic pollution
www.plasticoceans.org

World Oceans Day: Get involved with this global celebration every June 8 by planning an event.
www.worldoceansday.org

Sea Shepherd Conservation Society: A charitable organization fighting for the protection of marine life and ecosystems
seashepherd.org

Surfrider Foundation: An organization dedicated to the protection of the world's oceans and beaches
www.surfrider.org

ABOUT THE AUTHOR

Hello. This is me. I am Martin Dorey. I'm a surfer, writer, beach lover, and anti-plastic activist. I live near the sea in Cornwall, England, with my partner, Lizzy, who is also known as Dr. Seaweed. She's a gardener and botanist. My children, Maggie and Charlotte, live down the road from me with their dog, Bob, a medium-size pooch of unknown origin. They sometimes come beach-cleaning with me.

I have too many surfboards, a big camper van, and a bike that I enjoy riding down muddy hills with Dr. Seaweed. I like writing, camping, clean beaches, eating granola bars, and waking up to sunny days by the sea with the people I love the most.

ABOUT THE #2MINUTEBEACHCLEAN

The **#2minutebeachclean** is a campaign that began many years ago. After discovering an area of my local beach knee-deep in plastic bottles, I vowed, there and then, that I would do something, anything, to make a difference.

I set up the Beach Clean Network in 2009 and began using the **#2minutebeachclean** hashtag on social media in 2013. The idea is very simple: each time you go to the beach, you take two minutes to pick up beach litter, take a picture of it, and then post it to social media to inspire others to do the same. In 2014, the Beach Clean Network set up eight Beach Clean Stations around Cornwall that make it really easy for people to pick up litter at the beach. In 2019, there were more than five hundred litter-picking stations, with one of the most used in a school.

The **#2minutebeachclean** has now evolved to include the **#2minutelitterpick** and the **#2minutestreetclean**, as well as the **#2minutesolution**. On social media, we've seen that our thousands of followers are fighting plastic every day by cleaning beaches, picking up litter from the streets, or making plastic-free choices. All I ask is that you continue to take two minutes out of your day to pick up litter, make a change, or cut out plastic from your life. It might not seem like much, but when you add it to everyone else's efforts, it begins to make a big difference.

In 2019, the Beach Clean Network became a charity: The 2 Minute Foundation. Find out more: **www.beachclean.net**

With thanks to:
Lizzy;
Daisy, Maria, and all at Walker Books;
Nicky, Dolly, Andrea, Adam, Alan, Tab, and Jackie;
the **#2minutebeachclean** team
and the **#2minutebeachclean** family;
and Chris Hines.
My superheroes: Neil Hembrow (KBT), Deb Rosser (ReFILL South West), Rowena Bird (Lush), Rob Thompson (Ocean Recovery Project), Linda Thomas (Eco Design), Pete Cooper (the Crackington Crew), and the legendary Jim Scown (ex-RNLI)
Also: British Divers Marine Life Rescue, the Cornish Seal Sanctuary, Clive Symm, the Crackington Crew, Widemouth Task Force, the Plastic Movement, Surfers Against Sewage, Paddle Against Plastic, and all the amazing anti-plastic groups in the UK and beyond who are making a huge difference.